This book belongs to:
(Este libro pertenece a:)

For my little sissy,

This one is for you! - DLS

"Morning, Mr. Mustache! Time to go out and play.

I cannot wait, to explore all day!"

"¡Buenos días, Señor Bigote! Hora de ir a jugar.

Estoy ansiosa por explorar todo el día!"

"Just let me grab my magnifying glass and explorer sash!"

And DLee was up and out with a flash.

"¡Deja que tome mi lupa y mi cinto de explorador!"

Y DLee estuvo lista en un segundo.

"The countdown starts now.

Ready, set, Kapow!"

"El conteo empieza ahora.

¡En sus marcas, listos, vamos!"

Outside in the yard, DLee shouted,

"Look what I see!"

Afuera en el jardín, DLee gritó,

"¡Miren lo que estoy viendo!"

10

"Ten bluebirds chirping at me."

"Diez pajaritos azulejos cantando."

"With a hip and a hop, I see…"

"Doy un brinco y un salto para ver…"

9

"**N**ine butterflies flying up top."

"**N**ueve mariposas volando alto."

"Oh my! Oh why! Now I see…"

"¡Oh no! ¡Oh no! Ahora veo…"

8

"Eight bumble bees buzzing, oh geez!"

"¡Ocho abejitas zumbando!"

"And who can this be, oh I see..."

"Y quiénes pueden ser estas, ah ya veo..."

7

"Seven marching ants underneath the plants."

"Siete hormigas marchando bajo las plantas."

"With a whoop and a swoop, I see…"

"Doy un grito y salto cuando veo…"

6

"Six large beetles around my hula-hoop."

"Seis escarabajos alrededor de mi hula-hula."

"With a skip and a stop, I see…"

"Luego brinco y me detengo a ver…"

5

"Five small snails on the garbage pails."

"Cinco caracoles en los tarros de basura."

"I wonder what I will find next."

"Me pregunto ¿que mas ire a ver.?"

"Oh I see…"

"Ah, ya veo…"

4

"Four leap frogs jumping on some logs."

"Cuatro ranas saltando los maderos."

"As I whirl and I swirl, I see…"

"Dando vueltas y piruetas, miro…"

3

"Three baby squirrels, oh how I love to twirl!"

"Tres ardillitas, ¡oh me encanta hacer piruetas!"

"And high in the sky, I see…"

"Y en lo alto de los cielos puedo ver…"

2

"Two fireflies shining as bright as my eyes!"

"¡Dos luciérnagas brillantes como mis ojos!"

"With a turn of my head, I see…"

"Al voltear mi cabeza, veo…"

1

"One Daddy waving, DLee time for bed!"

"Un papá llamando, ¡DLee, es hora de dormir!"

If you liked this book, check out DLee in:

(Si te gustó este libro, echa un vistazo a DLee en:)

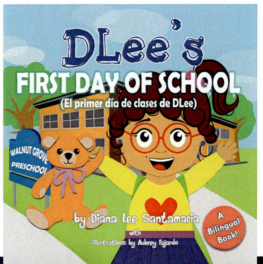

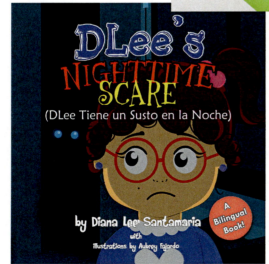

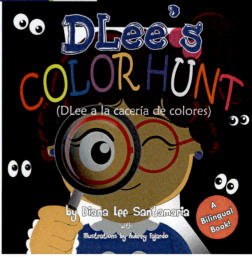

www.dleesworld.com

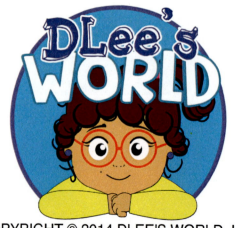

COPYRIGHT © 2014 DLEE'S WORLD, LLC.
ALL RIGHTS RESERVED.

Made in the USA
Middletown, DE
21 September 2017